GUENEVER SPEAKS

GUENEVER SPEAKS

by

Wendy Mnookin

Illustrations
by
Deborah Davidson

Round Table Publications
Rochester, NY
1991

ACKNOWLEDGMENTS

Earlier versions of "Guenever Plots Against Elaine," "Guenever Retreats to Almesbury," "Guenever Returns from the Garden," and "Guenever Views the Corpse of Elaine" were published in *The Round Table*.

"Guenever Loses Her Baby" was first published in *Without Child*, Ellen Sarasohn Glazer and Susan Lewis Cooper, eds. (Lexington: Lexington Books, 1988). Permission to reprint is gratefully acknowledged.

My thanks to Alan and Barbara Lupack for their continued encouragement of my work on Guenever.

And special thanks to Ruth Whitman, whose class inspired and nurtured these poems; to the women in my workshops at the Radcliffe Seminars, whose suggestions helped shape the poems; and to Anne Carroll Fowler, friend and poet, who knows Guenever well--maybe better than she wanted to.

ISBN 0-9630918-0-8

Round Table Publications
P. O. Box 18673
Rochester, NY 14618

For my children

Seth
Abigail
Jacob

ABOUT THE AUTHOR

Wendy Mnookin has had poetry published in various journals, including *Kalliope*, the *Beloit Poetry Journal*, *Cimarron Review*, *Passages North*, and the *Wisconsin Review*. She is the recipient of several prizes in national poetry competitions.

A graduate of Radcliffe College, Wendy Mnookin received her MFA in Writing from Vermont College in Montpelier, Vermont. She lives in Newton, Massachusetts with her husband, Jim, and their three children, Seth, Abigail and Jacob.

ABOUT THE ILLUSTRATOR

Deborah Davidson received her BA in Fine Arts from SUNY Binghamton and her MFA from Tufts University, School of the Museum of Fine Arts. She exhibits extensively and is currently producing monotypes, small scale sculpture and one-of-a-kind books. She lives in Somerville, Massachusetts.

Ms. Mnookin and Ms. Davidson work together frequently. They conduct workshops in the schools in poetry-writing and book-making and are currently collaborating on another book of poetry.

TABLE OF CONTENTS

PART ONE   1

Guenever Travels to Arthur   2
Guenever Waits for Arthur   3
Guenever Prays for a Child   5
Guenever Lies with Arthur   6
Guenever Pleads for Time   7
Guenever Leaves a Feast   8
Guenever Considers Endings   9

PART TWO   11

Guenever at the Table   12
Guenever Attends Tourneys at Surluse   13
Lancelot Comes to Guenever   14
Guenever Wants Her Reward   16
Guenever Listens to a Minstrel Sing of Love   18
Guenever Commands Lancelot to Leave Camelot   20
Guenever Goes Hawking After Lancelot's Departure   21
Guenever Greets Lancelot on His Return   22

PART THREE   23

Word of Lancelot Reaches Camelot   24
Guenever Finds Elaine's Token in Lancelot's Chamber   25
Guenever Plots Against Elaine   27
Guenever Views the Corpse of Elaine   28
Lancelot Departs on a Quest for the Grail   29
Guenever Celebrates Midsummer Eve Without Lancelot   30
Guenever Loses Her Baby   32
Guenever Hears of Lancelot's Penance for Their Love   35

PART FOUR   37

Guenever Is Accused of Poisoning Patrise   38
Lancelot Flees from Camelot   39
Guenever Listens to Arthur   40
Guenever Waits at Joyous Gard   41
Lancelot and Guenever Leave Joyous Gard   43
Guenever Retreats to Almesbury After Arthur's Death   44
Guenever in the Garden with Caroline   47
Guenever Returns from the Garden   48

EPILOGUE   50

PART ONE

"And so Leodegrance delivered
his daughter Guenever unto Merlin,
and the Table Round
with the hundred knights,

and so they rode freshly,
with great royalty,
what by water and what by land,
till that they came nigh unto London."

--Sir Thomas Malory, *Le Morte d'Arthur*

GUENEVER TRAVELS TO ARTHUR

In my father's kingdom the sun rose promptly
and travelled across the sky with purpose:
sunset, the reward of rest for a job well done.

Now the midday sun taunts me.
Glaring down from overhead, it creeps
like wagons laden with trunks and gifts,

ambling horses, bored knights, preening ladies--
who do not hurry towards a wedding at St. Stephen's,
and Arthur.

      in my tent this morning
        I waited for dawn
          inside the darkness

      I was a bride
        dressed in the gown
          packed in its own trunk

      a wife
        lying with Arthur
          clothed in his body

      a mother
        calling to her children
          Richard   Peter   Anne

      a Queen
        greeting her guests
          at the high table

Outside, rose seeped onto the horizon,
but the sun did not appear.
RISE, SUN! I commanded.

And it did.

GUENEVER WAITS FOR ARTHUR

My ladies remove my cloak,
ease velvet robes from my shoulders.
They dress me in a simple gown
and retire. Only Agnes remains.
She unplaits my hair
and brushes slowly, over and over,
one hand smoothing strands
that rise at her touch.
I stare into the fire,
watching sparks
until they disappear.

If I send her away
I could dress again in all my layers,
tie laces with elaborate care,
braid my hair tightly around gold threads.
Then would he take time?
Would he search with careful fingers
to undo the knots that bind me in my clothes?
Stone released sword so easily to his hands,
metal springing from granite at his touch--
could those hands work laces apart,
ease clothes from skin,
brush my hair?

GUENEVER PRAYS FOR A CHILD

St. Anne.
You knew emptiness,
                the years
of hollow longing.
Your prayers were answered.
Answer mine now.

Let it be tonight.

      Arthur.
      Our people marvel
      at your strength in battle.
      They travel far
      to seek your wisdom in court.
      You've performed miracles.
      Do this for me.

      Let it be tonight.

GUENEVER LIES WITH ARTHUR

In air heavy and dark as sea water,
we lie still waiting to see. Our eyes
search for form, breaking through dark
like shafts of sunlight slicing waves,
beams merging towards a distant depth,

but as my eyes find you, your eyes close
against me. Your hands slip from my face
to my breasts. Swimming in circles
traced by your fingers, I'm netted
by your touch, unable to break free

and unable to float towards you, snagged
as I wonder--has Merlin taught you
this touch? And what do you see
behind closed eyes? Do my colors fade,
eyes and hair shedding gold flecks

as they change into leaves and bark,
the forest where your men will gather?
Do you leave me for the dry land
of tomorrow's tournament? As we turn
my breast fills your hand--not enough

when there are empty seats at the Round Table.
So I close my eyes. When I smooth
the hair on the back of your neck
I stroke baby skin,
when you suck I want my milk to flow,

and when I open to receive you
I'm swimming free, gliding
down a sunlight shaft to a secret
underwater place where I wrap my legs
to trap your seed in me.

GUENEVER PLEADS FOR TIME

If I plead for time with you alone,
you'll grant me time
measured against tournaments, battles,

audience in court. If I ask you
to pick a four-leaf clover,
to hold it in your hand and see

the fairie world grown visible,
to watch with me as they dance
their fairie ring, to feel

the enchantment of their music
and their wings, you'll say *No*--
no four-leaf clovers

and wild fairie rings. Mortals
can be pulled into their midst
and vanish.

GUENEVER LEAVES A FEAST

Honored for his daring feats, Sir Tor
sits next to me at the high table.
We share a plate and cup

and I listen to his adventures through fourteen courses,
minstrels, jugglers, and a magician.
At meal's end servitors slash open

a huge pie, and a score of tiny birds flies out.
Dogs yelp and lunge, straining to get loose,
while birds circle higher and higher,

hoping for sky. A hawk is released.
Another. And another.
They reach the small birds quickly.

At the sound of falconers' bells
hawks drop their prey
and dogs are freed to retrieve the broken birds.

I reach for Arthur's arm.
"I need to rest," I say.
He escorts me to my room

as dogs go back to the scraps on the floor.

GUENEVER CONSIDERS ENDINGS

1.

I reach for Arthur's arm.
"I need to rest."
He escorts me to my room,
eases me into his lap.

He says nothing.
He smooths my hair,
rests his head on mine.
He rocks me back and forth

until I stop shaking.

2.

"I need to rest."
He escorts me to my room,
sends word to the hall
to excuse us.

"The birds," he says.
He puts his head in my lap.
He turns on his side,
draws his knees up.

He hides his eyes in my gown.

3.

He escorts me to my room.
His face is blank.
I don't know what he thinks.
Is he angry?

"I'll tell them you're ill,"
he says, and leaves.
I sink onto my bed,
close my eyes.

I watch the birds circle.

PART TWO

"Sir Lancelot du Lake passed all other knights
in tournaments and jousts and deeds of arms,
and at no time was he never overcome
but if it were by treason or enchantment.

Wherefore Queen Guenever had him in great favour
above all knights,
and in certain he loved the queen
above all other ladies of his life."

GUENEVER AT THE TABLE

When I first saw Arthur he looked like a boy--
thin, eager to fight, surprised at the victories
he always won. A King's daughter myself,
I knew greatness. I wanted to return to Camelot
as his Queen. Too much to hope for--

he returned to Camelot alone.
For months I prayed he would send for me.
When the messenger came I listened to my father
through the curtains--"best tidings I ever heard
that so worthy a King should wed my daughter."

Now I study Lancelot. He leans forward
at the table, one hand resting on his cup.
He raises the cup to his lips, looks at me.
This is no boy. I am no Princess, praying
to return to Joyous Gard as his wife. But

underneath the talk and laughter, I am praying.

GUENEVER ATTENDS TOURNEYS AT SURLUSE

The Haut Prince lets cry:
"Tourneys at Surluse for eight days!"
I go with thirty knights
and Lancelot. Arthur chooses
not to come.

For eight days of tourneys at Surluse
the horn blows to field
knights joust
I judge the winner
and the horn blows to lodging.

The tourneys at Surluse for eight days
have feasting and much merriment:
jugglers, acrobats, and one who swallows fire.
When Dinadan dresses as a maiden
I laugh until I have to leave the table.

For eight nights of tourneys at Surluse
I walk with Lancelot.
We talk, or walk in silence.
We never touch, not even
a careless brush of the shoulders.

LANCELOT COMES TO GUENEVER

not at Surluse
but here, here
you come to me
plead without words
with eyes, hands
pressing my skull
for thoughts
not spoken, seized
as you carve
the exact line
of my body
into stone

*

air
turns heavy
as water
clothes
weigh me down
arms and legs
tread in place:
breathe carefully
move slowly
go nowhere
wait
for night

*

burnt at the stake
for adultery
she choked
on black smoke
while I hid my eyes
in mother's gown
listening, imagining

hair singed
skin melting
mouth open wide
gulping
black air

GUENEVER WANTS HER REWARD

Arthur and I sit on our thrones.
The knights approach, one by one,
to tell us what they've done
and receive honors.

It takes forever.
It's hard to be still
and listen to their deeds--
joustings with evil knights,
dreadful wounds healed with magic salves,
and all those blonde maidens,
every one needful of rescue.

I can't add my deed to the list.
Arthur can't touch me
on the shoulder with his sword.
But I want my reward:

> To sit with Lancelot.
> To embrace him when he enters the room.
> To look straight at him and smile.
> To lean over and touch his arm.

> To sit with Lancelot.

GUENEVER LISTENS TO A MINSTREL SING OF LOVE

At ten, sewing,
pushing the needle in and out,
I looped the threads
    just so
and pulled them through:
    a petal.

Amazed, I tried again,
and again a petal,
raised and distinct,
    beautiful.
I did more and more,
    a field of petals.

"Mother!" I cried,
"look what I've done!
A new stitch--
    petals--"
I thrust the sewing at her
    for her praise.

She looked.
She smiled her grown-up smile
and bent her head towards me.
    "Petals.
How clever you are!
    But Guenever,

this isn't new.
It's called the *petal stitch*."
She kissed my head
    and walked away.
Others were in the room,
    witnesses.

I didn't cry.
Careful not to run

I left the room,
   no sorceress
of stitchery, just a girl
   who skipped one lesson.

GUENEVER COMMANDS LANCELOT TO LEAVE CAMELOT

...to keep you as a dream
of touch, vague as lashes
on a cheek, blurred
as light through closed
eyes; not the searing
of your fingers on my
skin, invisible marks
burning long after
you leave

GUENEVER GOES HAWKING AFTER LANCELOT'S DEPARTURE

Riding through woods, we search for herons.
My hawk rests on my gloved hand,
bells on his legs ringing softly.
He is hooded from sights, waiting.

A heron is spotted.
At a signal hawks are uncovered.
They race for the prey, the sound of bells
lost in the frantic beating of wings.

We chase the hawks, keeping them
in sight until the heron is captured.
We wheel sharply,
stop

I blow my small silver whistle
straightaway my hawk heads for me
a rush of air and flapping of wings
before he reaches my outstretched wrist

GUENEVER GREETS LANCELOT ON HIS RETURN

Candles
dyed with saffron
    release
scent of spices.
    Herbs float
in rosewater.
    Laurel
in the hearth burns
    slowly.
When you enter
    the air
stirs and a flame
    flickers.
I hold my breath
    and watch
as it straightens.
    I turn
to you, hold out
    yarrow.
I dip my hands
    in rose-
water and touch
    your face.

PART THREE

"Queen Guenever sent one of her women
unto Sir Lancelot's bed;
and when she came there
she found the bed cold.

Alas, said the Queen,
where is that false knight?
Then the Queen was nigh out of her wit,
and she writhed and weltered as a mad woman."

WORD OF LANCELOT REACHES CAMELOT

The court is loud

with news

of Lancelot's adventures:

at Corbin

he rescued a maiden

naked as a needle

        Elaine

young   rich   wise

        beautiful

and now heavy with his child.

My face aches from smiling.

GUENEVER FINDS ELAINE'S TOKEN
IN LANCELOT'S CHAMBER

Is it a gift for me?
I'm happy to take it!
I can't wear it on my sleeve
to champion her cause

but I can tuck it in my sleeve
to wipe tears.
                    Or we can play
blind man's bluff--
stand still
while I cover your eyes
and spin you around

you can't see
you're dizzy

where are you

GUENEVER PLOTS AGAINST ELAINE

She brings the child.
"I call him Galahad, your childhood name.
He'll be like you. Teach him well."

I wanted a child,
but prayed each month against this need,
against a revelation of our love.
Perhaps God heard--

I have no heir to carry on for Arthur.
No son for Lancelot to teach.
No daughter to reflect myself.
I have no child to brim me up.

I have only this love
Elaine means to steal.
Tonight she'll learn her place in his heart--
she'll wait for him in vain
while he lies in my arms.
I'll tell Arthur I'm unwell,
put Elaine down the hall,
Lancelot here--
                how I hate all this!
Arthur pulled sword from stone and became king.
A potion made Lancelot lie with Elaine.
Where's some magic now, for me?

I'll boil one horned lizard
with seven drops of blood, bright red,
at midnight pour it into earth
and say three times, "I want her dead."

I'll take two raven feathers,
three whiskers from the cat I found,
weave them tightly to my hair--
and Lancelot's forever bound.

GUENEVER VIEWS THE CORPSE OF ELAINE

Dressed in satins touched with lace,
she's pale against the black samite,
a solemn bride.
But Lancelot doesn't wait with a ring.
He offers the mass-penny.

Did I do this?

Lancelot.
I hardly dared wish for him.
Did she hope, as I did,
for just one touch,
her fingers through his hair?
When she feathered his hair
did she wish for an embrace,
his arms pressing the small of her back,
and then once to lie with him,
stretched against his length?
Did she long to see him vulnerable
in sleep?

Now she lies dead,
the funeral barge a mockery
of her wish for a marriage bed.
She holds a letter to Lancelot
locked in her hand:
bury me and pray for my soul.
Everyone cries and blames him.
Even I turn on him--*could you not love her?*--
grasping for a way out of what I know:
she was killed by a horned lizard
and seven drops of blood.

LANCELOT DEPARTS ON A QUEST FOR THE GRAIL

At the table a cracking and crying of thunder,
a sunbeam more clear than day by seven times,
a vessel covered with white samite.

Amazed, the knights want to see the vessel
uncovered, a privilege reserved for the holy.
All take vows and leave on quests,

Lancelot among them. As he rides away
I open my eyes wide to cup tears,
but tears spill over and I can't see.

I don't need to see the grail uncovered
or Lancelot ride away. I can imagine
the heavy silk falling from the urn,

Lancelot growing smaller,
a splash of color at the edge of the meadow.
How he turns, and disappears.

GUENEVER CELEBRATES MIDSUMMER EVE
WITHOUT LANCELOT

We join hands and circle the fire seven times,
moving slowly from east to west, like the sun.
Our voices rise together, chanting summer's riddles:
Green is gold, fortune is told,
fire is wet, dragon is met.
After the last turn I lead everyone away--

everyone but you. Since our quarrel you stayed away.
I wish we could start again, before the time
at Corbin. I wish you two had never met.
I wish she never had your son.
You crashed through the window when I told
you to be gone, and as you fled you sang in riddles:

When is love no longer love? Enough riddles!
Why do you run naked through the woods, keeping away
from the men I send to find you? I'm told
you wander aimlessly, day and night, all time
the same to you. You don't take shelter from the sun,
wind, or rain. What fate have you met?

I must know if you're alive. If we'll ever meet.
I crack the diviner's egg and look for riddles.
Your face in the yolk? The face of a son?
A daughter? Shapes take wishes' forms and fade away.
I try again, and again, but each time
it's unclear what future's been foretold.

Maybe St. John's bread. I've been told
you see what you want in the egg. I've met
those who saw gold coins during scarce times,
strong limbs when sick. I mustn't force the riddles.
I'll ask simply, *How long will he stay away?*
A clear question of number: *How many suns*

those who hate
Arthur and me
will watch her closely.

Green eyes or grey?
Red hair or brown?
Which one does she resemble?

Maybe me--
her mother's child
exposing no one

leaving me
always uncertain
whose child she is.

9 days late

I can't bear
the days of waiting
not knowing.

What if
she looks like Lancelot?
I must find out

what to do
how to shake her
loose.

No!

10 days late

I dream
    I'm a wild duck
        flying

Arthur
    sends his hawk
        to bring me down

I'm grabbed
    by the neck
        twisted

a whistle
    I fall down
        and down

I can't fly
    I drop
        to the ground

broken
    the dog's mouth
        closes on me

he brings me
    to his master
        Lancelot

I wake to blood

GUENEVER HEARS OF LANCELOT'S PENANCE
FOR THEIR LOVE

The hermit says you have no peer
in any earthly sinful man.
I can imagine how that fires you
to have no peer at all--
you hear mass daily and pray
not to fall to sin again.

That's me. I am your sin.
You cannot pray me away
and be chaste again,
but you try.
You refuse meat and wine,
wear hair from a holy man
against your skin.
Does that bring you closer
to your quest?
          Or maybe,
as you turn on your bed, restless
with pain, your mind slips
to other times, when gentle fingers
eased you into sleep.
Sinful thoughts, my love.
Fill your stomach with good food,
wear smooth silks next to your skin,
if penitence makes you long for me.

The hermit says
you have loved a queen unmeasurably
and out of measure long.
What does this hermit know,
who thinks God can be appeased
with simple food and daily masses?
I'd give alms until the coffers emptied,

shun feasts for bread and water,
I'd wear hairshirt, too,
if skin chafed raw with remorse
could buy ease.

Tell your holy man to let us be.
We have ways to torture body and soul
no simple hermit can devise.
When I lie in bed with Arthur,
trying to recall my young warrior,
I see instead your face above me.
I'm afraid when he touches me
I'll cry out your name,
or in my sleep I'll call for you.

When Arthur names you his most loyal knight--
his truest friend--
I see you pale.
Your jaw clenches tight.
Can this monk do better?

We have loved unmeasurably,
but not out of measure long.
Our time still spills before us.
Come home.
I'll rub balm into your chest
where penance pricks it sore,
salve your chafed back
and ease you into sleep again.

PART FOUR

"Great penance Guenever took,
as ever did sinful lady in this land.
Never creature could make her merry.

She lived in fasting, prayers and alms-deeds,
that all manner of people marvelled
how virtuously she was changed."

GUENEVER IS ACCUSED OF POISONING PATRISE

Mother, remember the ring?
I dressed up as Queen, my finger
so small your ring slipped off.

You never knew--
                    but days later
you punished me for stealing sweets.
I never touched them.

Forbidden from the feast, I wanted
to cry out, "It was the ring!
I lost the ring!"

as I want to cry out now
when Patrise falls from the table
and all eyes turn on me.

LANCELOT FLEES FROM CAMELOT

caught
in my chamber

Lancelot
kills
twelve knights

as I watch

red   washes   everywhere

Lancelot
pleads
with me
to flee with him

I am rooted
to the place
of devastation

GUENEVER LISTENS TO ARTHUR

These years I've wondered
if he knows. Now I see:
he has nurtured rage.

"I am more sorry by far
for my good knights' loss
than the loss of my fair Queen."

He has held his anger
close and warm, until it falls
overripe to the ground.

"Queens I might have enough
but such a fellowship of knights
will never come again."

I move aside, but *queens*
and *knights* smash at my feet
and break open. The rotten pulp

splashes the hem of my gown.

GUENEVER WAITS AT JOYOUS GARD

rescued

from the stake
taken to
Joyous Gard
where daily
Gawaine taunts
Lancelot

to fight

Arthur stands
with Gawaine
I fear soon
I must watch
Arthur and
Lancelot

at war

LANCELOT AND GUENEVER LEAVE JOYOUS GARD

I move slowly
in a sea of green:
a hundred knights in green velvet
all my ladies robed in green
green drapings on the horses
olive branches...

> tall grasses in the meadow
> where I played with my dog

> he held still, nose to the ground,
> rump in the air, until one of us

> broke loose and ran

I follow Lancelot back to Arthur.
We are silent.
There is nothing to say,
and everyone listens.
We alone are dressed in white,
woven with threads of gold...

> bright sun as I lay back
> and crowned Lancelot *my love*

> so bright when I looked up at him
> I could not see the woven flowers

> only a halo of light

We approach Arthur in silence.
In silence we dismount and kneel.
Lancelot gives me his arm
as we rise and face Arthur.
The silence is more deafening
than words.

GUENEVER RETREATS TO ALMESBURY
AFTER ARTHUR'S DEATH

      The sisters say walk,
walk in the garden.
So I do. I work in the garden,
raking fingers through thick blankets of thyme,
pinching off tops of basil. Smell
makes me dizzy. I hold my head.
Fingers smell rich.

> *spice fingers*
> *unsullied with food*
> *saved for dipping*
> *in cinnamon*
>   *sweet basil*
>   *honey*
>
> *but I don't dip*
> *I save the smell of you*
> *on fingers*

I thin the sage and tie up mint.

> *fresh rushes*
> *on the floors*
> *at festivals*
>   *roses*
>   *lilies*
>   *mint*
>
> *but the soft crush*
> *turns brittle*
>   *filthy*

There are weeds,
more weeds than I can pull.
And I am late for prayers.

      The sisters say read,
why don't you read?

I have your letter
in the pages of my Bible.

Guenever
in you I have my earthly joy
leave Almesbury now
and be with me

The words tilt on the page.
I turn my head, follow them
up
      down.
I snap the book shut
to keep the words still.

do not write
no use in sending letters
I cannot read them

I will not read your letters

  The sisters say rest,
get some sleep.
I lie awake and wait for Matins.

awake
I do not see
Gaheris and Gareth
unarmed
     slain
by you in my rescue

The nuns return from morning prayers
to sleep. Three hours until Prime.
Three hours to lie awake.

entombed
a stone house built around her:
Crazy Anne: killed her husband

eyes closed
I see you
fighting Arthur lying dead

Air cuts my eyes
like broken glass.
I will not close my eyes.

   The sisters say eat,
you must eat to stay well.
I move the food around and smile.

Yesterday I swooned at Vespers.
I must eat some bread.
A little bread
so I won't swoon.
So I can stay awake.

lying in bed
hip bones push
against skin

it is my time
I bleed

GUENEVER IN THE GARDEN WITH CAROLINE

As she bends over books
her eyes wash over,
her mouth just opens.
Caroline comes each day
with the other girls
to study with the sisters,
but she does not learn to read,
she cannot write her name.

I shape a stem of grass
into a *C*. A fish in the pond
makes an *O* and disappears.
As we lie on our backs
and stare at the sky
we see that the clouds,
hiding from the sun all day,
have come out
to write the letters of her name.

GUENEVER RETURNS FROM THE GARDEN

Sister Margaret and I
walk with Caroline
back from the garden.

We walk in silence,
although now I speak.
There is little need

for talk,
and the sisters observe
silence.

Caroline skips ahead.
Her hair floats
up

   and down

        until she's lost
in leaves
as she rounds
a tree
   my eyes strain
to find her
I see the bough
that closed
around her
     leaves
orange
   gold

but Caroline is gone

leaves
where hair should be
I see red

black

Sister Margaret eases me
down
I breathe
in gasps
          a voice
from far away
a voice
I do not recognize
                my voice
speaks
of things I have not said before

Margaret listens.
It grows late, and cold,
and still she listens.

My voice comes back
from far away.
My breath comes easy.

When I'm done speaking
we sit in silence
for a long time.

Then I say,
just under the quiet,
"I will stay at Almesbury

until I die.
I cannot look
at Lancelot's face

again.
I cannot lose him
again."

EPILOGUE

"Hither he cometh as fast as he may.
Wherefore I beseech Almighty God--

may I never have the power
to see Lancelot
with my worldly eyen.

And thus was ever her prayer
these two days
until she was dead. *"*